A New Twist

Turn 6 Easy Blocks into
12 Colorful Quilts

Nancy Mahoney

Martingale®
Create with Confidence

A New Twist: Turn 6 Easy Blocks into 12 Colorful Quilts
© 2022 by Nancy Mahoney

Martingale®
18939 120th Ave. NE, Ste. 101
Bothell, WA 98011-9511 USA
ShopMartingale.com

Printed in Hong Kong
27 26 25 24 23 22   8 7 6 5 4 3 2 1

Library of Congress Cataloging-in-Publication Data is
available upon request.

ISBN: 978-1-68356-176-7

MISSION STATEMENT

We empower makers who use fabric and yarn
to make life more enjoyable.

CREDITS

**PUBLISHER AND
CHIEF VISIONARY OFFICER**
Jennifer Erbe Keltner

CONTENT DIRECTOR
Karen Costello Soltys

DESIGN MANAGER
Adrienne Smitke

TECHNICAL EDITOR
Ellen Pahl

PRODUCTION MANAGER
Regina Girard

COPY EDITOR
Melissa Bryan

**COVER AND
BOOK DESIGNER**
Mia Mar

ILLUSTRATOR
Sandy Loi

PHOTOGRAPHER
Brent Kane

SPECIAL THANKS
*Some of the photography for this book was taken at
the home of Tracie Fish of Kenmore, Washington.*

Contents

Introduction

Over the 40 years I've been making quilts, I have come to realize that my favorite quilts are scrappy ones made with traditional blocks. In this book, you'll find instructions for making six scrappy quilts using traditional, asymmetrical blocks. Included in each project is a second scrappy quilt made from the same block but with different colors and the blocks turned to create a totally different design. All of the quilts feature a side-by-side setting, with no sashing or alternate blocks. Asymmetrical blocks create exciting and surprising secondary designs that come to life as the individual boundaries of blocks disappear and an overall design emerges.

These stash-busting quilts are perfect for beginners who are learning to quilt and for more experienced quilters who want to use their stash. Although the quilts look complex, they are easy to make using half-square-triangle units, four-patch units, stitch-and-flip techniques, or simple foundation piecing.

So, if you love scrap quilts and traditional blocks, now is the time to grab your scrap basket and start stitching.

~ Nancy

Make It Scrappy

I love quilts where every block is constructed of different fabrics. More is better! Scrap quilts are more interesting when you use prints that vary in scale and texture. I make sure to include large- and small-scale prints, as well as stripes, dots, florals, and geometric prints. I also use prints of different values within each color family, such as light, medium, and dark green prints. A variety of prints makes the quilt sparkle and keeps your eyes moving around the quilt to discover hidden secondary designs.

Much has been written about selecting fabrics for a scrap quilt, but don't get bogged down trying to follow rules. The problem with rules is that you can generally find an exception to each one. So rather than give you a set of rules, I will provide some guidelines and three scrap plans that I find helpful when making scrap quilts.

Fabric Selection

To build your skill in selecting fabrics, start by looking at lots of scrap quilts in books and at quilt shows. Make notes of what you like and what you think doesn't work well. Then consider the following guidelines and the scrap plans beginning on page 8 as you make choices about color and fabrics.

- Choose colors according to value. The lightness or darkness of a color is more important than the color itself. If your quilt seems lifeless, it probably needs more contrast between the fabrics. Contrast can make or break a quilt; without sufficient contrast the patchwork design gets lost. To create more contrast, add a fabric that is lighter or darker or brighter.

- Stretch the range of colors within a color group. "Red" can include everything from rusty brown to scarlet to reddish purple.

- Add dimension to your quilt with fabrics that vary in intensity. More intense colors will stand out and advance toward the viewer. Bright, clear colors are high in intensity, while muted or grayed colors are low in intensity.

- Use a variety of scales and textures to make your quilt interesting. Florals, plaids, stripes, and geometric designs in different scales can all work together in a quilt. Include a few novelty prints to add a little surprise for the viewer.

- Think of blending the fabrics instead of matching them exactly. Don't scrutinize each print too carefully. Scrap quilts are more intriguing if the fabrics aren't too closely coordinated.

- Incorporate neutral colors, such as white, beige, cream, gray, or even black to give your eye a place to rest. Cream or white will make the design look crisp and clean. Black will make the other colors glow.

The individual blocks featured in this book can all be made with a fat quarter (18" × 21") or less of each print. For some of the quilts, the amount listed in "Materials" indicates the total amount of assorted prints needed for each color. The actual amount needed of each print will vary depending on the number of fabrics you decide to use. I look for fat quarters and fat eighths (9" × 21") in my local quilt shop and online. I also purchase precut squares in a variety of sizes. This allows me to add small pieces of fabrics to my stash that I might not buy otherwise.

Glossary of Terms

Color Family: A category comprising fabrics that are all the same color but have different values, textures, scale, and intensity.

Contrast: The evident difference between two or more fabrics placed side by side.

Intensity: The strength or brightness of a color.

Monochromatic: Colors from one color family.

Scale: The relative size of a motif in printed fabric.

Value: The lightness or darkness of a fabric.

Visual Texture: The pattern printed on a fabric.

Scrap Plans

To make it easier for quilters of all skill levels to create a successful scrap quilt, I've come up with three basic scrap plans that anyone can follow for the design they want to make and the scraps they have available. Remember, for any of the scrap plans to be successful, you need a good measure of prints that vary in value, intensity, scale, and visual texture, which are all discussed on pages 6 and 7.

Unlimited Scrap Plan

The unlimited scrap plan is just what it sounds like—it accommodates any color, so there really are no limits. Using many colors and print styles can be fun and a great way to clear out your scrap bin, but planning this type of quilt can be intimidating. Here are some tips I use that make this process easier:

- Don't try to coordinate fabrics for the whole quilt at once. Instead, try choosing colors or fabrics for one block at a time.

- Instead of placing specific colors in the same spot in each block, simply assign values of light and dark. That way, instead of having all the greens in one spot and all the blues in another, you can place any dark color in the spots assigned to be darks.

- Use a consistent color for the background. This doesn't mean you have to limit yourself to one fabric, but rather you can use scraps of many fabrics as long as they are in the same color family, such as all whites or all pale blues. This will give your quilt a more cohesive look regardless of whether you use 25 scraps or 250 scraps.

The blocks in Boxed Jewels (below and page 57) feature a different dark print for each block, but I used the same light print for all of the patches.

Limited Scrap Plan

Many quilters find it easier to make the transition to scrap quilting by using a limited palette of scraps. The quilt will have a similar feel to one made of three or four fabrics; you simply replace each individual fabric with scraps in the same colors. So, if quilts made with unlimited scrap colors are too flamboyant or intimidating for you, you may find it easier to use a limited scrap plan. Your quilt will still look scrappy and have lots of visual interest, but your fabric choices will be more controlled. Here are some pointers for working in a limited scrap plan:

- Try using a common background fabric or a neutral color for all of the background areas.

- Limit the color palette to three or four colors, such as the red, black, and white On the Road quilt (below and page 19). Using both dark and light neutral colors like black and white sets the stage for scraps of your favorite color to shine.

- When you're ready to expand, you can use multiple colors in place of the main color, replacing the red scraps in On the Road with assorted bright colors to build your comfort level with scrap quilting.

On the Road (below and page 19) has both a limited color palette and specific color placement. The quilt features three colors, although a wide range of values is used within each color. The reds range from a dark red to a brighter red-orange. The black prints include gray motifs as well as black motifs. The light background ranges from bright white to cream. The black and gray prints also range in value and texture. Notice that the red, light, and black prints are used in the same position in each block.

Two-Color Scrap Plan

While this is the most limited version of all the scrap plans, a two-color quilt can be very dramatic. Mix in many values, textures, scales, and intensities of those two colors and the quilt will be bursting with dimension and appeal. Typically, a two-color plan consists of a main color and a background color. But remember, limiting the colors doesn't mean limiting the fabrics. Rather, think of using a wide range of the main color and blending the fabrics. Up close, you may feel that true red and red-orange clash, but when you also incorporate brick red, cherry red, coral red, and so on, you'll soon see how these all work together. Here are some tips to help you get started:

- Just because you've limited the color choices doesn't mean you should limit the fabric choices. In my Flying in Formation quilt pictured below right and on page 16, I used 120 different red prints. The more the merrier!

- Don't worry about all the shades of your main color scraps matching. If you wanted them to match, you could use a single fabric instead of scraps.

- Think about making the background areas scrappy too. You may not have as many lights (or maybe blacks!) as you have of your main color, but it's fun to collect them as you visit quilt shops or to trade among your friends.

Lime Saltwater Taffy (above and page 34) uses a neutral palette with an accent color. Various medium and dark gray prints (from 36 fat eighths) along with 18 different green prints are used for the blocks. The background consists of at least 18 similar light prints in silver. The contrast between the light prints and darker gray fabrics adds dimension to the design.

Flying in Formation (above and page 16) includes a variety of red prints and a range of cream prints. Did you notice how the lighter and brighter prints add life to the quilt? High contrast between the red prints and the cream background makes the quilt seem to vibrate and glow.

In Flight

Flock of Geese is a versatile block that creates a multitude of designs. For this quilt, join blocks into four identical quadrants and then rotate the quadrants so that the triangles (or geese) appear to radiate from the center outward. Not all geese fly south!

Finished quilt: 70½" × 70½" / Finished block: 8" × 8"

Materials

Yardage is based on 42"-wide fabric.

* 3⅓ yards *total* of assorted white tone on tones for blocks
* 3⅓ yards *total* of assorted color prints for blocks
* ⅜ yard of yellow print for inner border
* 1⅛ yards of aqua dot for outer border and binding
* 4⅓ yards of fabric for backing
* 77" × 77" piece of batting

Cutting

All measurements include ¼" seam allowances.

From the assorted white tone on tones, cut a *total* of:
256 squares, 3" × 3"
64 squares, 5" × 5"

From the assorted color prints, cut a *total* of:
256 squares, 3" × 3"
64 squares, 5" × 5"

From the yellow print, cut:
7 strips, 1½" × 42"

From the aqua dot, cut:
7 strips, 2½" × 42"
8 strips, 2¼" × 42"

Making the Blocks

Press seam allowances in the directions indicated by the arrows.

1 Draw a diagonal line from corner to corner on the wrong side of the white 3" squares. Layer a marked square on a print 3" square, right sides together. Sew ¼" from both sides of the drawn line. Cut the unit apart on the marked line to make two half-square-triangle units. Trim the units to 2½" square, including seam allowances. Make 512 units.

Make 512 units.

2 Lay out four of the triangle units in two rows of two. Sew the units into rows. Join the rows to make a four-patch unit measuring 4½" square, including seam allowances. Make 128 units.

Make 128 units,
4½" × 4½".

3 Draw a diagonal line from corner to corner on the wrong side of the white 5" squares. Layer a marked square on a print 5" square, right sides together. Sew ¼" from both sides of the drawn line. Cut the unit apart on the marked line to make two half-square-triangle units. Trim the units to 4½" square, including seam allowances. Make 128 units.

Make 128 units.

4 Lay out two four-patch units from step 2 and two triangle units from step 3 in two rows of two, orienting the units as shown. Sew the units into rows. Join the rows to make a Flock of Geese block measuring 8½" square, including seam allowances. Make 64 blocks.

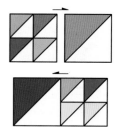 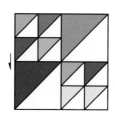

Make 64 blocks,
8½" × 8½".

Unlimited Scrap Plan

When following this plan, it's easiest to first assign light and dark fabric positions within the block. For In Flight, all of the light fabrics are white tone-on-tone prints. The darks feature a variety of bright colors, both multicolored prints and tone on tones. The dark fabrics also include dots, stripes, florals, and novelty prints to add visual texture.

Pieced by Nancy Mahoney; quilted by Mary Frost

In Flight

Assembling the Quilt Top

1 Lay out 16 blocks in four rows of four blocks each. Sew the blocks into rows. You may need to re-press some of the final seam allowances in the blocks to create opposing seams. Join the rows to make a quadrant. Make four quadrants measuring 32½" square, including seam allowances.

Make 4 quadrants,
32½" × 32½".

Keep It Simple

Sewing the blocks into quadrants makes it easier to be sure all the blocks are positioned correctly. Another benefit is that you will only have to sew one long seam to complete the quilt top, which makes assembly a breeze.

2   Lay out the quadrants, rotating them as shown in the quilt assembly diagram below. Sew the quadrants into rows. Join the rows to make the quilt-top center, which should measure 64½" square, including seam allowances.

3   Join the yellow strips end to end. From the pieced strip, cut two 66½"-long strips and two 64½"-long strips. Sew the shorter strips to opposite sides of the quilt center. Sew the longer strips to the top and bottom edges. The quilt top should measure 66½" square, including seam allowances.

4   Join the aqua 2½"-wide strips end to end. From the pieced strip, cut two 70½"-long strips and two 66½"-long strips. Sew the shorter strips to opposite sides of the quilt center. Sew the longer strips to the top and bottom edges. The quilt top should measure 70½" square.

Finishing the Quilt

For more details on any finishing steps, visit ShopMartingale.com/HowtoQuilt for free downloadable information.

1   Layer the quilt top with batting and backing; baste the layers together.

2   Quilt by hand or machine. The quilt shown is machine quilted with an allover design of swirls and circles.

3   Use the aqua 2¼"-wide strips to make double-fold binding. Attach the binding to the quilt.

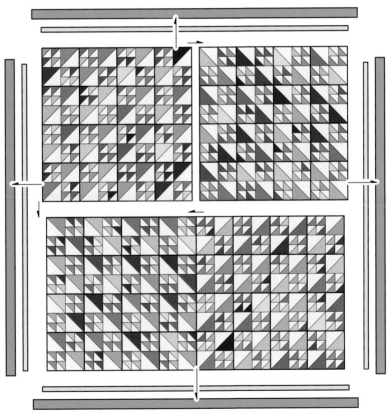

Quilt assembly

Flying in Formation

In this new twist on In Flight, all the Flock of Geese blocks use just two colors: red and cream. When the blocks are rotated and set in alternating directions, an entirely different design of diamond shapes emerges.

Finished quilt: 70½" × 70½" / Finished block: 8" × 8"

Pieced by Nancy Mahoney; quilted by Mary Frost

Materials

Yardage is based on 42"-wide fabric.

❋ 3⅓ yards *total* of assorted cream prints for blocks

❋ 3⅓ yards *total* of assorted red prints for blocks

❋ ⅞ yard of red print for inner border and binding

❋ ⅝ yard of cream print for outer border

❋ 4⅜ yards of fabric for backing

❋ 77" × 77" piece of batting

Cutting

All measurements include ¼" seam allowances.

From the assorted cream prints, cut a *total* of:
256 squares, 3" × 3"
64 squares, 5" × 5"

From the assorted red prints, cut a *total* of:
256 squares, 3" × 3"
64 squares, 5" × 5"

From the red print for inner border and binding, cut:
7 strips, 1½" × 42"
8 strips, 2¼" × 42"

From the cream print for outer border, cut:
7 strips, 2½" × 42"

Two-Color Plan

Although I used an assortment of red prints that range from dark red to bright red to blue-red and orange-red, this quilt design essentially requires two values: dark and light. You can easily substitute another color in place of red to make this quilt your own. What color do you have the most of in your stash? Whether it's red, blue, or something else, it would be a good starting point for Flying in Formation.

Assembling and Finishing the Quilt

Press seam allowances in the directions indicated by the arrows.

1 Referring to "Making the Blocks" (page 11) for detailed instructions and illustrations, use the cream and red squares to make 64 Flock of Geese blocks.

2 Lay out the blocks in eight rows of eight blocks each, rotating the blocks as shown in the quilt assembly diagram on page 18. Sew the blocks into rows and then join the rows. The quilt-top center should measure 64½" square, including seam allowances.

3 Join the red 1½"-wide strips end to end. From the pieced strip, cut two 66½"-long strips and two 64½"-long strips. Sew the shorter strips to opposite sides of the quilt center. Sew the longer strips to the top and bottom edges. The quilt top should measure 66½" square, including seam allowances.

4 Join the cream strips end to end. From the pieced strip, cut two 70½"-long strips and two 66½"-long strips. Sew the shorter strips to

opposite sides of the quilt center. Sew the longer strips to the top and bottom edges. The quilt top should measure 70½" square.

5 Layer the quilt top with batting and backing; baste the layers together. Quilt by hand or machine. The quilt shown is machine quilted with allover feather plumes and swirls. Use the red 2¼"-wide strips to make double-fold binding and then attach the binding to the quilt.

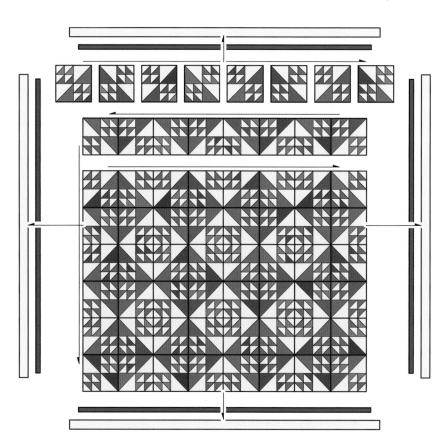

Quilt assembly

A New Twist

On the Road

Blend three distinct colors to create visual pop in the traditional Road to Oklahoma blocks. Sort your scraps into reds, blacks, and whites to begin this road trip and take your scrap bins out for a spin!

Finished quilt: 43½" × 55½" / Finished block: 6" × 6"

Materials

Yardage is based on 42"-wide fabric.

- ½ yard of white solid for blocks
- 48 squares, 5" × 5" *each*, of assorted red prints for blocks
- 24 pieces, 5" × 9" *each*, of assorted medium to dark gray and black prints for blocks (collectively referred to as "black")*
- 24 squares, 5" × 5" *each*, of assorted dark gray and black prints for blocks (collectively referred to as "black")
- 96 squares, 5" × 5" *each*, of assorted white prints for blocks
- ⅔ yard of black print for inner border and binding
- ½ yard of white stripe for outer border
- 2⅞ yards of fabric for backing
- 50" × 62" piece of batting

Gray is a tint of black.

Cutting

All measurements include ¼" seam allowances.

From the white solid, cut:
  6 strips, 2" × 42"; crosscut into 96 squares, 2" × 2"

From *each* of the red print squares, cut:
  4 squares, 2" × 2" (192 total)

From *each* of the 5" × 9" black print pieces, cut:
  8 squares, 2" × 2" (192 total)

From *each* of the 5" × 5" black print squares, cut:
  4 squares, 2" × 2" (96 total)

From *each* of the white print squares, cut:
  2 pieces, 2" × 3½" (192 total)

From the black print for inner border and binding, cut:
  5 strips, 1½" × 42"; crosscut *2 of the strips* into 2 strips, 1½" × 38½"
  6 strips, 2¼" × 42"

From the white stripe, cut:
  5 strips, 3" × 42"

Making the Blocks

Press seam allowances in the directions indicated by the arrows.

1 Lay out two white solid and two red squares in two rows of two. Sew the squares together into rows. Join the rows to make a four-patch unit measuring 3½" square, including seam allowances. Make 48 units.

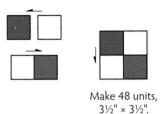

Make 48 units,
3½" × 3½".

2 Draw a diagonal line from corner to corner on the wrong side of 192 black 2" squares. Place a marked black square on one end of a white print 2" × 3½" piece, right sides together. Sew on the marked line. Trim the excess corner fabric, ¼" from the stitched line, to make a star-point unit. Reverse the placement of the black square, noting the direction of the marked line, to make a reversed unit. Make 96 of each unit.

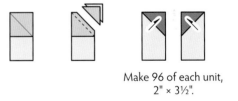

Make 96 of each unit,
2" × 3½".

3 Lay out two red squares, two black squares, two of each black star-point unit, and one four-patch unit in three rows, rotating the star-point units as shown. Sew the squares and units into rows. Join the rows to make a Road to Oklahoma

block. Make 48 blocks measuring 6½" square, including seam allowances.

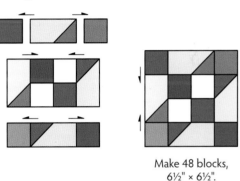

Make 48 blocks,
6½" × 6½".

Limited Scrap Plan

I used a limited color palette and specific color placement to create this quilt. The three colors are red, black, and white. The whites consist of many prints as well as white solid. Each color is used in the same position in each block, with the white solid used in each of the four-patch units. Red and black appear in a wide array of values, including gray, which is a tint of black. A medley of scale and texture in all colors adds interest.

Pieced by Nancy Mahoney; quilted by Karen Hodge

A New Twist

Skip the Line

If you want to avoid drawing lines to make the star-point units, try a specialty ruler such as a Folded Corner Clipper tool from Creative Grids, designed by Susan Nelson, or a Mini Simple Folded Corners ruler by Doug Leko. Simply layer a square on one end of a rectangle with right sides together and raw edges aligned. Use the ruler to trim the corner, being sure to follow the manufacturer's instructions. Then sew along the angled edge using a ¼" seam allowance. Voilà!

Assembling the Quilt Top

1 Lay out the blocks in eight rows of six blocks each, rotating the blocks to form stars as shown in the quilt assembly diagram on page 24. Sew the blocks into rows. Join the rows to make the quilt-top center, which should measure 36½" × 48½", including seam allowances.

2 Join the remaining black 1½" × 42" strips end to end. From the pieced strip, cut two 48½"-long strips and sew them to opposite sides of the quilt top. Sew the black 38½"-long strips to the top and bottom edges. The quilt top should measure 38½" × 50½", including seam allowances.

3 Join the white stripe 3"-wide strips end to end. From the pieced strip, cut two 50½"-long strips and two 43½"-long strips. Sew the longer strips to opposite sides of the quilt top. Sew the shorter strips to the top and bottom edges. The quilt top should measure 43½" × 55½".

Finishing the Quilt

For more details on any finishing steps, visit ShopMartingale.com/HowtoQuilt for free downloadable information.

1 Layer the quilt top with batting and backing; baste the layers together.

2 Quilt by hand or machine. The quilt shown is custom machine quilted with straight lines in the red and black pieces. Curved lines are stitched in the background area. A wavy line is stitched in the inner border and straight lines are stitched in the outer border.

3 Use the black 2¼"-wide strips to make double-fold binding. Attach the binding to the quilt.

Quilt assembly

A New Twist

Crisscrossed Paths

The Road to Oklahoma blocks take a one-way approach with this new twist—each block is heading in the same direction. Keep the three-color combination of fabrics, but note how the stars disappear and the chains take on a contrasting look.

Finished quilt: 43½" × 55½" / Finished block: 6" × 6"

Pieced and quilted by Nancy Mahoney

Materials

Yardage is based on 42"-wide fabric.

- 1½ yards of white solid for blocks
- ¾ yard *total* of assorted green prints for blocks
- 1¼ yards *total* of assorted light, medium, and dark purple prints for blocks
- ¼ yard of lime green print for inner border
- ½ yard of orchid print for outer border
- ½ yard of violet print for binding
- 2⅞ yards of fabric for backing
- 50" × 62" piece of batting

Cutting

All measurements include ¼" seam allowances.

From the white solid, cut:
23 strips, 2" × 42"; crosscut into:
192 pieces, 2" × 3½"
96 squares, 2" × 2"

From the assorted green prints, cut a *total* of:
192 squares, 2" × 2"

From the assorted purple prints, cut a *total* of:
288 squares, 2" × 2"

From the lime green print, cut:
5 strips, 1½" × 42"; crosscut *2 of the strips* into
2 strips, 1½" × 38½"

From the orchid print, cut:
5 strips, 3" × 42"

From the violet print, cut:
6 strips, 2¼" × 42"

Assembling and Finishing the Quilt

Press seam allowances in the directions indicated by the arrows.

1 Referring to "Making the Blocks" (page 21) for detailed instructions and illustrations, use the white, green, and purple pieces to make 48 blocks.

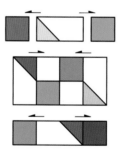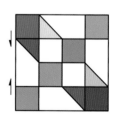

Make 48 blocks,
6½" × 6½".

2 Lay out the blocks in eight rows of six blocks each as shown in the quilt assembly diagram on page 27. Sew the blocks into rows and then join the rows. The quilt-top center should measure 36½" × 48½", including seam allowances.

Limited Scrap Plan

When you work with a limited scrap plan, as was done here, make sure that you incorporate numerous darker prints as well as a potpourri of lighter (or lilac) prints. If you don't want to stray too far, you can limit your choices to dark and medium values, as was done with the greens in this quilt. Placing the same color/shade in the same position in each block helps balance the look of the quilt.

quilt center. Sew the lime 38½"-long strips to the top and bottom edges. The quilt top should measure 38½" × 50½", including seam allowances.

4 Join the orchid strips end to end. From the pieced strip, cut two 50½"-long strips and two 43½"-long strips. Sew the longer strips to opposite sides of the quilt center. Sew the shorter strips to the top and bottom edges. The quilt top should measure 43½" × 55½".

5 Layer the quilt top with batting and backing; baste the layers together. Quilt by hand or machine. The quilt shown is machine quilted with loops and feathers in the blocks, swirls in the inner border, and straight lines in the outer border. Use the violet 2¼"-wide strips to make double-fold binding and then attach the binding to the quilt.

3 Join the remaining lime 1½" × 42" strips end to end. From the pieced strip, cut two 48½"-long strips and sew them to opposite sides of the

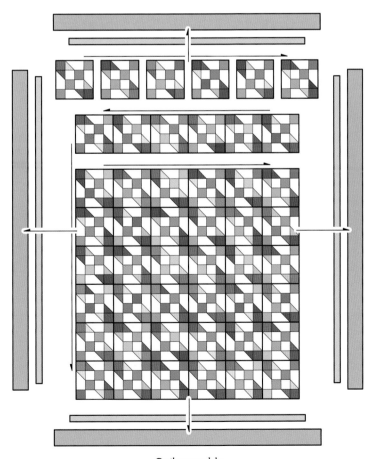

Quilt assembly

Crisscrossed Paths

Hard Candy

Like a kid in a candy store, have fun choosing assorted flavors (um, prints) for a vibrant throw. Strategically placed black prints shift the focus to the hourglass shapes formed where four Hovering Hawks blocks meet.

Finished quilt: 79½" × 79½" / Finished block: 12" × 12"

Materials

Yardage is based on 42"-wide fabric. Fat eighths measure 9" × 21".

* 1⅞ yards of white solid for blocks
* 27 fat eighths of assorted black prints for blocks
* 1 piece, 8" × 12", *each* of 108 assorted color prints for blocks
* ½ yard of black solid for inner border
* ¾ yard of teal print for outer border
* ⅝ yard of purple print for binding
* 7⅜ yards of fabric for backing
* 88" × 88" piece of batting

Cutting

All measurements include ¼" seam allowances.

From the white solid, cut:
15 strips, 4" × 42"; crosscut into 144 squares, 4" × 4". Cut *72 of the squares* in half diagonally to yield 144 triangles.

From *each* of the assorted black print fat eighths, cut:
4 squares, 4" × 4" (108 total)

From *each of 36* assorted color print pieces, cut:
1 square, 6⅞" × 6⅞"; cut the square in half diagonally to yield 2 triangles (72 total)
1 square, 4" × 4" (36 total)

From *each of the remaining 72* assorted color print pieces, cut:
2 squares, 3½" × 3½" (144 total)

From the black solid, cut:
8 strips, 1½" × 42"

From the teal print, cut:
8 strips, 3" × 42"

From the purple print, cut:
9 strips, 2¼" × 42"

Unlimited Scrap Plan

Need help getting started on a super scrappy quilt? Begin by pulling a random collection of bright print fabrics that include dots, stripes, florals, and novelty prints. The bright prints should vary in value and intensity. To create more contrast, choose an assortment of black tone-on-tone prints for the framework and a white solid for the background to give your eyes a place to rest.

Pieced by Nancy Mahoney; quilted by Terri Taylor

A New Twist

Making the Blocks

Press seam allowances in the directions indicated by the arrows.

1 Draw a diagonal line from corner to corner on the wrong side of the white 4" squares. Layer a marked square on a black 4" square, right sides together. Sew ¼" from both sides of the drawn line. Cut the unit apart on the marked line to make two half-square-triangle units. Trim the units to 3½" square, including seam allowances. Make 144 white/black units.

3½"

3½"

Make 144 units.

2 Draw a diagonal line from corner to corner on the wrong side of the assorted color 4" squares. Repeat step 1 using the marked squares and the remaining black squares to make 72 assorted color/black units.

3½"

3½"

Make 72 units.

3 Lay out two white/black units and two assorted color 3½" squares in two rows of two, referring to the diagram. Sew the units and squares into rows. Join the rows to make an A unit measuring 6½" square, including seam allowances. Make 72 units.

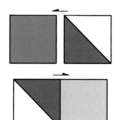 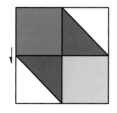

Make 72 A units,
6½" × 6½".

4 Sew a short side of a white triangle to each color print side of a unit from step 2 to make a triangle unit. Make 72 units. Align the 45° line on a ruler with a short side of each unit; trim the unit, making sure to leave ¼" beyond the seam intersection for seam allowances.

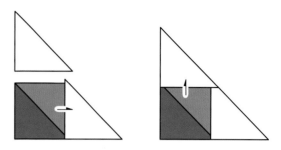

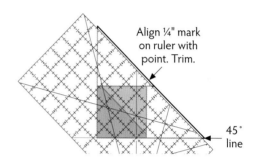

Align ¼" mark on ruler with point. Trim.

45° line

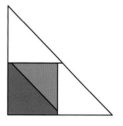

Make 72 units.

5 Sew a print triangle to the long side of a triangle unit from step 4 to make a B unit measuring 6½" square, including seam allowances. Make 72 units.

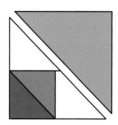 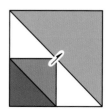

Make 72 B units,
6½" × 6½".

6 Lay out two A and two B units in two rows of two units each, rotating the units so that the black triangles form a diagonal pattern. Sew the units into rows. Join the rows to make a Hovering Hawks block measuring 12½" square, including seam allowances. Make 36 blocks.

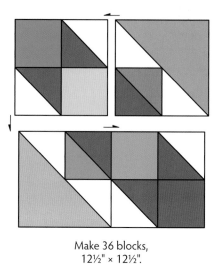

Make 36 blocks,
12½" × 12½".

Pressing Matters

When assembling the blocks, here's how you can create opposing seams and reduce bulk where the four seams meet. After sewing the rows together, use a seam ripper to remove one or two stitches from the seam allowance. Gently reposition the seam allowances to evenly distribute the fabric. Press the seam allowances in opposite directions.

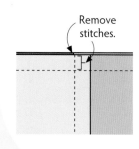

Remove stitches.

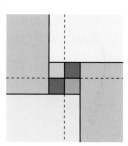

Assembling the Quilt Top

1. Lay out the blocks in six rows of six blocks each, rotating every other block as shown in the quilt assembly diagram below. Sew the blocks into rows. Join the rows to make the quilt-top center, which should measure 72½" square, including seam allowances.

2. Join the black solid 1½"-wide strips end to end. From the pieced strip, cut two 74½"-long strips and two 72½"-long strips. Sew the shorter strips to opposite sides of the quilt center. Sew the longer strips to the top and bottom edges. The quilt top should measure 74½" square, including seam allowances.

3. Join the teal 3"-wide strips end to end. From the pieced strip, cut two 79½"-long strips and two 74½"-long strips. Sew the shorter strips to opposite sides of the quilt center. Sew the longer strips to the top and bottom edges. The quilt top should measure 79½" square.

Finishing the Quilt

For more details on any finishing steps, visit ShopMartingale.com/HowtoQuilt for free downloadable information.

1. Layer the quilt top with batting and backing; baste the layers together.

2. Quilt by hand or machine. The quilt shown is machine quilted with an allover design of swirls and bubbles.

3. Use the purple 2¼"-wide strips to make double-fold binding. Attach the binding to the quilt.

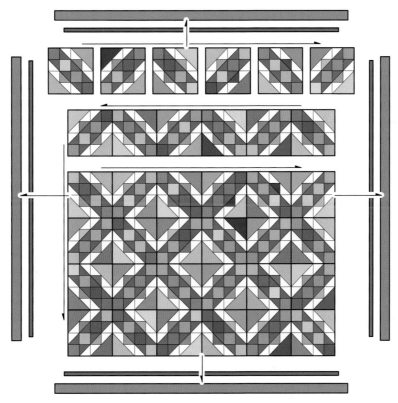

Quilt assembly

Hard Candy

Lime Saltwater Taffy

Go row by row for this new twist on Hard Candy. Alternating the direction of the Hovering Hawks blocks by row removes the hourglass shapes altogether and results in a zigzag pattern you may love even more!

Finished quilt: 79½" × 79½" / Finished block: 12" × 12"

Pieced by Nancy Mahoney; quilted by Terri Taylor

Materials

Yardage is based on 42"-wide fabric. Fat quarters measure 18" × 21"; fat eighths measure 9" × 21".

- 18 fat eighths of assorted green prints for blocks
- 36 fat eighths of assorted medium and dark gray prints for blocks (collectively referred to as "gray")
- 18 fat quarters of assorted light gray and silver prints for blocks (collectively referred to as "silver")
- 1 yard of charcoal print for inner border and binding
- ¾ yard of pewter print for outer border
- 7⅜ yards of fabric for backing
- 88" × 88" piece of batting

Cutting

All measurements include ¼" seam allowances.

From *each* of the assorted green print fat eighths, cut:

6 squares, 4" × 4" (108 total)

From *each* of the assorted gray print fat eighths, cut:

1 square, 6⅞" × 6⅞"; cut the square in half diagonally to yield 2 triangles (72 total)

2 squares, 4" × 4" (72 total)

2 squares, 3½" × 3½" (72 total)

From *each* of the assorted silver print fat quarters, cut:

6 squares, 4" × 4"; cut *4 of the squares* in half diagonally to yield 8 triangles (144 total)

4 squares, 3½" × 3½" (72 total)

From the charcoal print, cut:

8 strips, 1½" × 42"

9 strips, 2¼" × 42"

From the pewter print, cut:

8 strips, 3" × 42"

Limited Scraps Plan

When you're trying to achieve movement in a geometric design, consistent color placement across the quilt top is often the key. To do this, assign each color a position in the block. Play with color schemes and placement until you're happy with the overall look. Make a few test blocks and photograph them with your phone to compare them. A computer program for designing quilts can be helpful, or use graph paper and colored pencils to sketch your design.

Assembling and Finishing the Quilt

Press seam allowances in the directions indicated by the arrows. Refer to "Making the Blocks" (page 31) for additional instructions.

1. Draw a diagonal line from corner to corner on the wrong side of the green 4" squares. Make 144 green/gray half-square-triangle units and 72 green/silver half-square-triangle units.

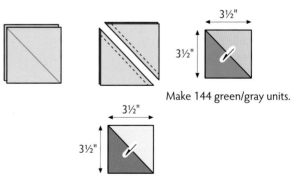

Make 144 green/gray units.

Make 72 green/silver units.

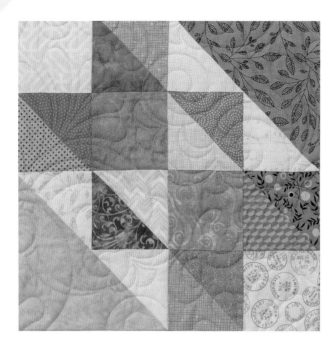

4 Sew a gray triangle to the long side of a triangle unit from step 3 to make a B unit. Make 36 units with a dark gray triangle and 36 with a medium gray triangle.

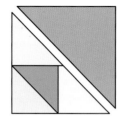
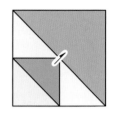

Make 36 dark gray B units,
6½" × 6½".

Make 36 medium gray B units,
6½" × 6½".

2 Lay out two green/gray half-square-triangle units, one gray 3½" square, and one silver 3½" square as shown. Sew together to make an A unit. Make 72 units.

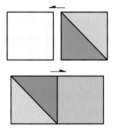
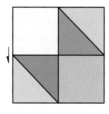

Make 72 A units,
6½" × 6½".

5 Lay out two A and two B units as shown and sew together to make the block. Make 36 blocks.

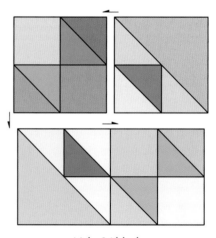

Make 36 blocks,
12½" × 12½".

3 Sew two silver triangles to the green print side of a green/silver unit as shown. Make 72 units and trim as instructed in step 4 on page 31.

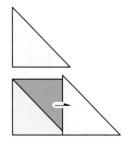
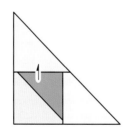

Make 72 units.

6 Lay out the blocks in six rows of six blocks each, rotating the blocks in every other row as shown in the quilt assembly diagram on page 37. Sew the blocks into rows and then join the rows. The quilt-top center should measure 72½" square, including seam allowances.

A New Twist

7 Join the charcoal 1½"-wide strips end to end. From the pieced strip, cut two 74½"-long strips and two 72½"-long strips. Sew the shorter strips to opposite sides of the quilt center. Sew the longer strips to the top and bottom edges. The quilt top should measure 74½" square, including seam allowances.

8 Join the pewter strips end to end. From the pieced strip, cut two 79½"-long strips and two 74½"-long strips. Sew the shorter strips to opposite sides of the quilt center. Sew the longer strips to the top and bottom edges. The quilt top should measure 79½" square.

9 Layer the quilt top with batting and backing; baste the layers together. Quilt by hand or machine. The quilt shown is machine quilted in an allover design of plumes and swirls. Use the charcoal 2¼"-wide strips to make double-fold binding and then attach the binding to the quilt.

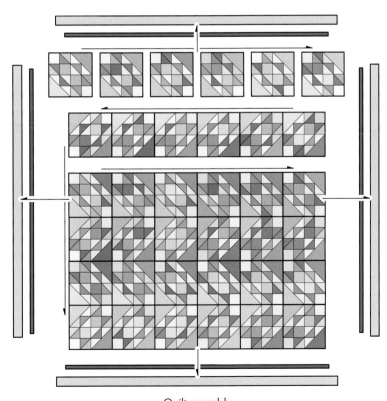

Quilt assembly

Lime Saltwater Taffy

Flying Home

Small in size but big on style, Flying Geese blocks can be a breeze to make using paper foundation piecing. Give the technique a whirl and see how satisfying those precise points can be.

Finished quilt: 43½" × 43½" / Finished block: 5" × 5"

Materials

Yardage is based on 42"-wide fabric.

- 1⅞ yards of ivory solid for blocks
- 2⅞ yards *total* of assorted medium and dark prints for blocks (collectively referred to as "dark")
- ¾ yard of pink print for border and binding
- 2⅞ yards of fabric for backing
- 50" × 50" piece of batting
- Papers for foundation piecing*
- Water-soluble glue stick
- 1" × 6" ruler or 6" Add-A-Quarter ruler
- 3" × 5" piece of cardstock

*I use Martingale's Papers for Foundation Piecing, available wherever you buy quilt books and notions. They come in packages of 100 sheets that you can use in a printer or photocopier.

Cutting

All measurements include ¼" seam allowances.

From the ivory solid, cut:

21 strips, 2¾" × 42"; crosscut into 288 squares, 2¾" × 2¾". Cut the squares in half diagonally to yield 576 triangles.

From the dark prints, cut a *total* of:

64 squares, 5" × 5"; cut the squares in half diagonally to yield 128 triangles

160 squares, 3" × 3"; cut the squares in half diagonally to yield 320 triangles

From the pink print, cut:

5 strips, 2" × 42"

5 strips, 2¼" × 42"

Unlimited Scrap Plan

The great thing about working with 1930s reproduction prints is that most of the value-sorting work has already been done. These prints are predominantly mid-range values, regardless of color, so mixing all the colors and prints is easy. If you wish to include some of the darker '30s prints, like the reds, dark purples, and blues I used, just use them more sparingly and sprinkle their placement across the quilt top for a good balance.

Making the Blocks

Press seam allowances toward each newly added triangle.

1 Make 64 copies of the foundation pattern on page 47. Trim the foundation papers ¼" from the outer (cutting) line.

2 Use the ivory triangles and an assortment of dark prints in each block as follows.

> **Pieces 1, 3, 4, 6, 7, 9, 10, 12, and 13:** ivory triangles
>
> **Pieces 2, 5, 8, 11, and 14:** dark 3" triangles
>
> **Pieces 15 and 16:** dark 5" triangles

3 Turn the foundation so that the blank (unmarked) side of the paper faces up. Using a water-soluble glue stick, apply a dab of glue in the center of area 1. Position the ivory triangle for piece 1, right side up, to cover area 1. Using the light source from your sewing machine, look through the fabric and paper to make sure area 1 is completely covered, plus a ¼" seam allowance around the entire area.

4 Place the dark 3" triangle for piece 2 on top of piece 1, right sides together. Holding the layers in place, carefully position the unit under your sewing machine's presser foot, printed side up. Shorten the stitch length to about 1.8, or 15 to 17 stitches per inch. Sew directly on the line between areas 1 and 2, starting ¼" before the line and extending ¼" beyond.

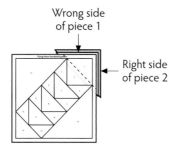

Wrong side of piece 1

Right side of piece 2

5 Open piece 2. Holding the unit up to the light, look through the fabric to make sure the edges of piece 2 extend beyond the seamlines for area 2. Refold the fabrics with right sides together and then fold the paper back to reveal the seam allowance. Place a 1" × 6" ruler along the edge of the paper and trim the seam allowance to ¼" if needed.

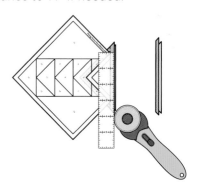

6 Open the fabrics so that both pieces are right side up and press the seam allowances to one side with a dry iron.

7 With the foundation on top, place the piece of cardstock on the line between pieces 2 and 3 and fold the paper back along the cardstock to expose the seam allowance. Place a ruler on the fold and trim the excess fabric so that it extends ¼" from the folded line. This trimming creates a straight edge upon which you can line up your next fabric piece, making placement much easier.

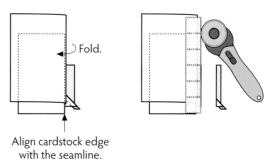

Fold.

Align cardstock edge with the seamline.

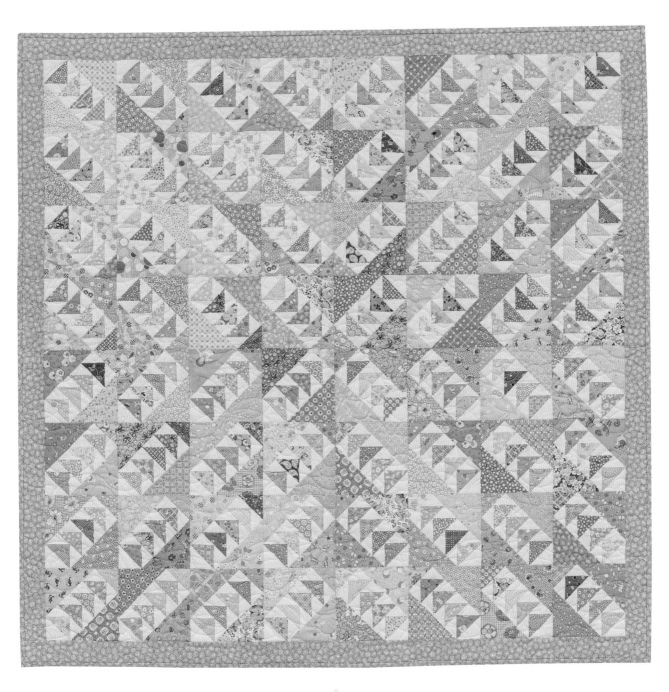

Pieced by Nancy Mahoney; quilted by Terri Taylor

Flying Home

8 Align an ivory triangle for piece 3 with the newly cut edge of piece 2, right sides together. Sew directly on the line between areas 2 and 3 in the same manner as before. Trim and press.

9 Continue adding pieces in numerical order and trimming until the foundation pattern is completely covered with fabric pieces. With the foundation on top, use a rotary cutter and ruler to trim the foundation and fabrics ¼" from the sewing line on all sides. The block should measure 5½" square, including seam allowances. Make 64 Flying Geese blocks and carefully remove the paper foundation from each.

Make 64 blocks,
5½" × 5½".

Paper Piecing

You can find additional details about my foundation piecing techniques in my book *Learn to Paper Piece: A Visual Guide to Piecing with Precision* (Martingale, 2016).

A New Twist

Assembling the Quilt Top

Press seam allowances in the directions indicated by the arrows.

1 Lay out the blocks in eight rows of eight blocks each, rotating the blocks as shown in the quilt assembly diagram below. Sew the blocks into rows. Join the rows to make the quilt-top center, which should measure 40½" square, including seam allowances.

2 Join the pink 2"-wide strips end to end. From the pieced strip, cut two 43½"-long strips and two 40½"-long strips. Sew the shorter strips to opposite sides of the quilt center. Sew the longer strips to the top and bottom edges. The quilt top should measure 43½" square.

Finishing the Quilt

For more details on any finishing steps, visit ShopMartingale.com/HowtoQuilt for free downloadable information.

1 Layer the quilt top with batting and backing; baste the layers together.

2 Quilt by hand or machine. The quilt shown is machine quilted with an allover design of swirls and flowers.

3 Use the pink 2¼"-wide strips to make double-fold binding. Attach the binding to the quilt.

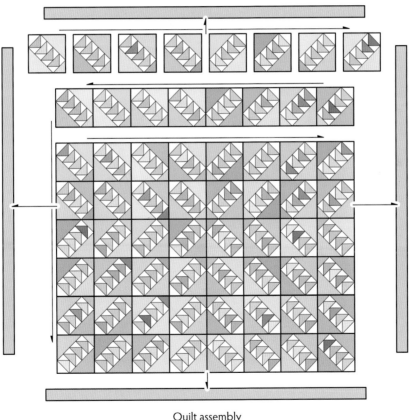

Quilt assembly

A Wreath of Geese

For this twist on Flying Home, the blocks feature a wide variety of bright prints. Pairing them with black and light prints not only gives a dramatic framework to the design, but also gives your eyes a place to rest. The blocks are set to create a ring around the center diamond for a quilt with maximum impact.

Finished quilt: 43½" × 43½" / Finished block: 5" × 5"

Pieced by Nancy Mahoney; quilted by Karen Hodge

Materials

Yardage is based on 42"-wide fabric. Fat quarters measure 18" × 21".

- 18 fat quarters of assorted light prints for blocks
- 40 squares, 8" × 8" *each*, of assorted dark prints for blocks
- 32 squares, 5" × 5" *each*, of assorted black prints for blocks
- ¾ yard of black tone on tone for border and binding
- 2⅞ yards of fabric for backing
- 50" × 50" piece of batting
- Papers for foundation piecing
- Water-soluble glue stick
- 1" × 6" ruler or 6" Add-A-Quarter ruler
- 3" × 5" piece of cardstock

Cutting

All measurements include ¼" seam allowances.

From *each* of the assorted light print fat quarters, cut:

16 squares, 2¾" × 2¾"; cut the squares in half diagonally to yield 32 triangles (576 total)

2 squares, 5" × 5"; cut the squares in half diagonally to yield 4 triangles (72 total; 8 will be extra)

From *each* of the assorted dark print squares, cut:

4 squares, 3" × 3"; cut the squares in half diagonally to yield 8 triangles (320 total)

From *each* of the assorted black print squares, cut in half diagonally to yield:

2 triangles (64 total)

From the black tone on tone, cut:

5 strips, 2" × 42"
5 strips, 2¼" × 42"

Unlimited Scrap Plan

Sometimes working with an unlimited amount of colors can feel overwhelming, but when you pair colors and prints that run the gamut with both black and light prints, it becomes much easier to see where the colors need to go to make the design work. This makes color placement decisions so much easier. For something completely different, consider using just three colors, such as red geese, white backgrounds, and blue frames. Or use a softer color palette, such as pink, cream, and chocolate brown.

Assembling and Finishing the Quilt

When piecing the blocks, press seam allowances toward each newly added triangle; when assembling the quilt top, press seam allowances in the directions indicated by the arrows.

1 Referring to "Making the Blocks" (page 40) for detailed instructions and illustrations, use the following pieces to make 64 blocks.

Pieces 1, 3, 4, 6, 7, 9, 10, 12, and 13: light 2¾" triangles

Pieces 2, 5, 8, 11, and 14: dark triangles

Piece 15: light 5" triangle

Piece 16: black triangle

3 Lay out the blocks in eight rows of eight blocks each, rotating the blocks as shown in the quilt assembly diagram below. Sew the blocks into rows and then join the rows. The quilt-top center should measure 40½" square, including seam allowances.

4 Join the black 2"-wide strips end to end. From the pieced strip, cut two 43½"-long strips and two 40½"-long strips. Sew the shorter strips to opposite sides of the quilt center. Sew the longer strips to the top and bottom edges. The quilt top should measure 43½" square.

5 Layer the quilt top with batting and backing; baste the layers together. Quilt by hand or machine. The quilt shown is machine quilted in the ditch around the geese. The light triangles feature a leaf design while the dark triangles are stitched in a geometric design of three irregular triangle shapes. The border is quilted in a zigzag chain. Use the black 2¼"-wide strips to make double-fold binding and then attach the binding to the quilt.

2 Trim and square up the blocks to 5½" square, including seam allowances.

Make 64 blocks,
5½" × 5½".

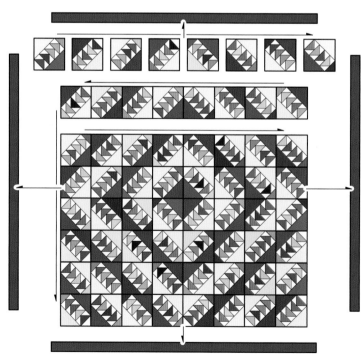

Quilt assembly

A New Twist

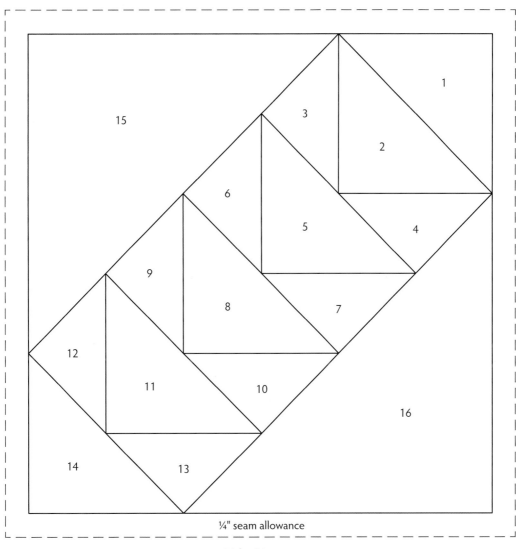

¼" seam allowance

Make 64 copies.

Scotch Plaid

Who doesn't love an easy-peasy block? Especially when the result looks much more complicated than it is! This variation of the traditional Scotch block includes a triangle unit that adds visual interest and keeps the eye moving over the design.

Finished quilt: 53½" × 53½" / Finished block: 6" × 6"

Materials

Yardage is based on 42"-wide fabric.

- 1¼ yards of ivory batik for blocks and inner border
- 3 yards *total* of assorted dark batiks for blocks and outer border
- ½ yard of black batik for binding
- 3⅜ yards of fabric for backing
- 60" × 60" piece of batting

Cutting

All measurements include ¼" seam allowances.

From the ivory batik, cut:

4 strips, 4" × 42"; crosscut into 32 squares, 4" × 4"

7 strips, 2" × 42"; crosscut into 128 squares, 2" × 2"

5 strips, 1½" × 42"

From the assorted dark batiks, cut a *total* of:

32 squares, 4" × 4"

128 pieces, 2" × 5"

128 pieces, 2" × 3½"

40 pieces, 2" × 5½"

4 squares, 2" × 2"

From the black batik, cut:

6 strips, 2¼" × 42"

Unlimited Scrap Plan

This quilt is the perfect opportunity to use all your leftover bits and pieces. I think of this design as using all the crayons in the box! Incorporating an ivory batik as a unifying fabric in each block gives a bit of structure to the layout and allows the bright colors to shine.

Pieced by Nancy Mahoney; quilted by Mary Frost

A New Twist

Making the Blocks

Press seam allowances in the directions indicated by the arrows.

1 Draw a diagonal line from corner to corner on the wrong side of the ivory 4" squares. Layer a marked square on a dark 4" square, right sides together. Sew ¼" from both sides of the drawn line. Cut the unit apart on the marked line to make two half-square-triangle units. Trim the units to 3½" square, including seam allowances. Make 64 units.

3½"

3½"

Make 64 units.

2 Lay out two dark 2" × 3½" pieces, one ivory 2" square, and one half-square-triangle unit in two rows. Sew the pieces into rows. Join the rows to make a unit measuring 5" square, including seam allowances. Make 64 units.

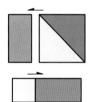

Make 64 units,
5" × 5".

3 Lay out two dark 2" × 5" pieces, one ivory 2" square, and one unit from step 2 in two rows. Sew the pieces into rows. Join the rows to make a Scotch block measuring 6½" square, including seam allowances. Make 64 Scotch blocks.

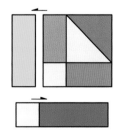 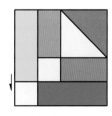

Make 64 blocks,
6½" × 6½".

Assembling the Quilt Top

1 Lay out the blocks in eight rows of eight blocks each, rotating every other block as shown in the quilt assembly diagram on page 52. Sew the blocks into rows. Join the rows to make the quilt-top center, which should measure 48½" square, including seam allowances.

2 Join the ivory 1½"-wide strips end to end. From the pieced strip, cut two 50½"-long strips and two 48½"-long strips. Sew the shorter strips to opposite sides of the quilt center. Sew the longer strips to the top and bottom edges. The quilt top should measure 50½" square, including seam allowances.

3 Join 10 dark 2" × 5½" pieces to make a side border measuring 2" × 50½", including seam allowances. Make two. Make two more borders in the same way and add a dark 2" square to each end. The top and bottom borders should measure 2" × 53½", including seam allowances.

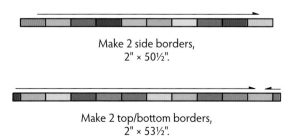

Make 2 side borders,
2" × 50½".

Make 2 top/bottom borders,
2" × 53½".

4 Sew the 50½"-long pieced borders to opposite sides of the quilt top. Sew the 53½"-long pieced borders to the top and bottom edges to complete the quilt top. The quilt top should measure 53½" square.

Finishing the Quilt

For more details on any finishing steps, visit ShopMartingale.com/HowtoQuilt for free downloadable information.

1 Stitch around the perimeter of the quilt top, ⅛" from the outer edges, to lock the seams in place.

2 Layer the quilt top with batting and backing; baste the layers together.

3 Quilt by hand or machine. The quilt shown is machine quilted with an allover design of swirls, leaves, and flowers.

4 Use the black 2¼"-wide strips to make double-fold binding. Attach the binding to the quilt.

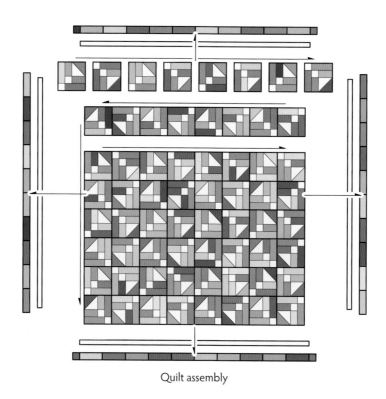

Quilt assembly

Colorful Windowpanes

In this twist on Scotch Plaid, two simple changes create an entirely different look. Notice how substituting black print triangles for assorted batik ones and setting the blocks so all triangles point toward the center makes it seem like you're peering at a black-and-white Barn Raising quilt through colorful windowpanes.

Finished quilt: 53½" × 53½" / Finished block: 6" × 6"

Pieced by Nancy Mahoney; quilted by Karen Hodge

From the light print for inner border, cut:
5 strips, 1½" × 42"

From the black print for binding, cut:
6 strips, 2¼" × 42"

Limited Scrap Plan

Scraps in this version of Scotch Plaid are limited to bright prints, light prints, and assorted black prints. I positioned each category in the same specific position within each block. The inclusion of the black prints adds depth and creates an exciting secondary design.

Materials

Yardage is based on 42"-wide fabric.

- 1 yard *total* of assorted light prints for blocks
- ⅝ yard *total* of assorted black prints for blocks
- 2⅝ yards *total* of assorted medium and dark prints for blocks and outer border (collectively referred to as "dark")
- ⅓ yard of light print for inner border
- ½ yard of black print for binding
- 3⅜ yards of fabric for backing
- 60" × 60" piece of batting

Cutting

All measurements include ¼" seam allowances.

From the assorted light prints, cut a *total* of:
32 squares, 4" × 4"
128 squares, 2" × 2"

From the assorted black prints, cut a *total* of:
32 squares, 4" × 4"

From the assorted dark prints, cut a *total* of:
128 pieces, 2" × 5"
128 pieces, 2" × 3½"
40 pieces, 2" × 5½"
4 squares, 2" × 2"

Assembling and Finishing the Quilt

Press seam allowances in the directions indicated by the arrows.

1 Referring to "Making the Blocks" (page 51) for detailed instructions and illustrations, use the light, black, and dark pieces to make 64 blocks.

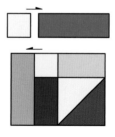 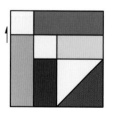

Make 64 blocks,
6½" × 6½".

2 Lay out the blocks in eight rows of eight blocks each, rotating the blocks as shown in the quilt assembly diagram below to form the black center diamond and echoing black triangles. Sew the blocks into rows and then join the rows. The quilt-top center should measure 48½" square, including seam allowances.

3 Join the light 1½"-wide strips end to end. From the pieced strip, cut two 50½"-long strips and two 48½"-long strips. Sew the shorter strips to opposite sides of the quilt center. Sew the longer strips to the top and bottom edges. The quilt top should measure 50½" square, including seam allowances.

4 Referring to step 3 of "Assembling the Quilt Top" on page 51, make two 50½"-long outer borders and sew them to opposite sides of the quilt top. Make two 53½"-long outer borders and sew them to the top and bottom edges. The quilt top should measure 53½" square.

5 Stitch around the perimeter of the quilt top, ⅛" from the outer edges, to lock the seams in place.

6 Layer the quilt top with batting and backing; baste the layers together. Quilt by hand or machine. The quilt shown is machine quilted in an allover design of leaves and swirls. Use the black 2¼"-wide strips to make double-fold binding and then attach the binding to the quilt.

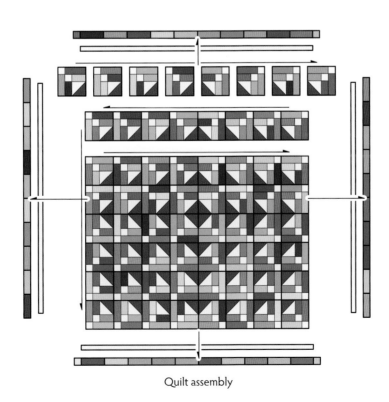

Quilt assembly

Boxed Jewels

The many names for this block include Buckeye Beauty, Going to Chicago, Jacob's Ladder, and Railroad Crossing. Although the blocks result in a quilt that looks complex, they are constructed of only two units—four patches and half-square triangles. This scrappy quilt is perfect for precuts!

Finished quilt: 48½" × 48½" / Finished block: 4" × 4"

Materials

Yardage is based on 42"-wide fabric.

- 144 squares, 5" × 5" *each*, of assorted light prints for blocks
- 180 squares, 5" × 5" *each*, of assorted color prints for blocks
- 1⅛ yards of white print for blocks
- ½ yard of rust print for binding
- 3 yards of fabric for backing
- 55" × 55" piece of batting

Cutting

All measurements include ¼" seam allowances.

From *each* of the assorted light print squares, cut:
  1 square, 3" × 3" (144 total)

From the assorted color print squares, cut a *total* of:
  144 squares, 3" × 3"
  576 squares, 1½" × 1½"

From the white print, cut:
  23 strips, 1½" × 42"; crosscut into 576 squares, 1½" × 1½"

From the rust print, cut:
  6 strips, 2¼" × 42"

Unlimited Scrap Plan

Don't let working with so many colors and prints mystify you. Simply assign dark and light values to each of the spots in your quilt block. Here, I used one white print for all the four-patch units, and filled in the other light areas with assorted light prints. Then I could randomly use any bright-color scrap for the darks. There's no need to fuss about which color is next to another color. You can just pick a print, sew it, and move on to the next one in random fashion. The result will be a colorful jewel box!

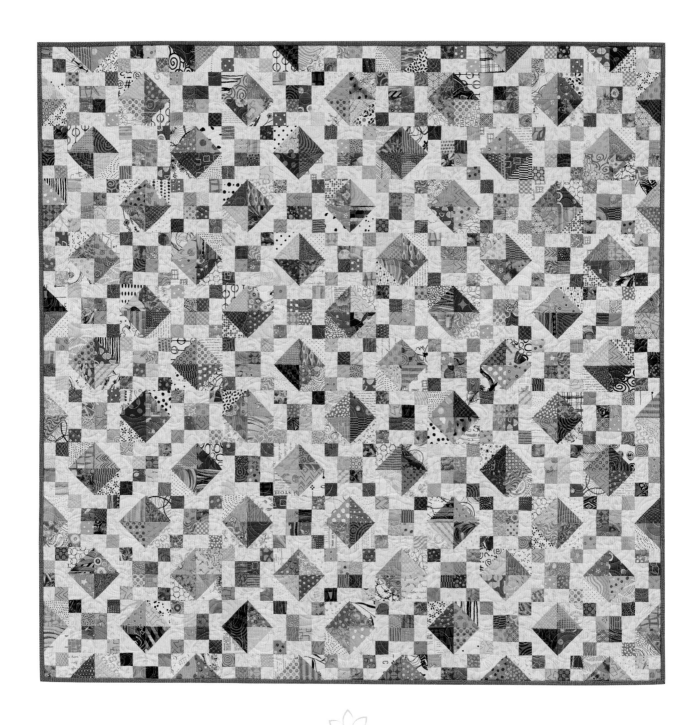

Pieced by Nancy Mahoney; quilted by Terri Taylor

A New Twist

Making the Blocks

Press seam allowances in the directions indicated by the arrows.

1 Draw a diagonal line from corner to corner on the wrong side of the light 3" squares. Layer a marked light square on a color print 3" square, right sides together. Sew ¼" from both sides of the drawn line. Cut the unit apart on the marked line to make two half-square-triangle units. Trim the units to 2½" square, including seam allowances. Make 288 units.

Make 288 units.

2 Lay out two white and two assorted color 1½" squares in two rows of two squares each. Sew the squares into rows. Join the rows to make a four-patch unit measuring 2½" square, including seam allowances. Make 288 units.

Make 288 units,
2½" × 2½".

3 Lay out two four-patch units and two half-square-triangle units in two rows of two. Sew the units into rows. Join the rows to make a Jacob's Ladder block measuring 4½" square, including seam allowances. Make 144 blocks.

Make 144 blocks,
4½" × 4½".

Keeping Track

To keep your blocks in the proper order when moving a row from the design wall to your sewing machine, try this. Write numbers 1 through 12 on flat-head pins using a permanent marker. Then insert a pin in the top of each block in numerical order. Chain piece the blocks, sewing block 1 to block 2, block 3 to block 4, and so on. Clip the threads between the blocks, and then sew block 2 to block 3, block 6 to block 7, and so on. Once all the blocks are joined into a row, press the seam allowances as instructed. Then use the pins for assembling the blocks in the next row. Note that you can also purchase flat-head pins that are already numbered.

Assembling the Quilt Top

Lay out the blocks in 12 rows of 12 blocks each, rotating every other block as shown in the quilt assembly diagram below. Sew the blocks into rows. Join the rows to complete the quilt top, which should measure 48½" square.

Finishing the Quilt

For more details on any finishing steps, visit ShopMartingale.com/HowtoQuilt for free downloadable information.

1 Stitch around the perimeter of the quilt top, ⅛" from the outer edges, to lock the seams in place.

2 Layer the quilt top with batting and backing; baste the layers together.

3 Quilt by hand or machine. The quilt shown is machine quilted with an allover design of swirls and bubbles.

4 Use the rust 2¼"-wide strips to make double-fold binding. Attach the binding to the quilt.

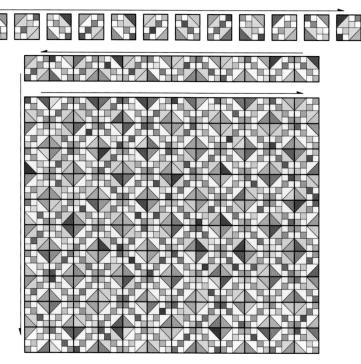

Quilt assembly

Faceted Jewels

Have fun putting a new twist on Jacob's Ladder blocks. Rotate them in the quilt layout to create a burst of color radiating from the center, adding facets of color in each corner.

Finished quilt: 48½" × 48½" / Finished block: 4" × 4"

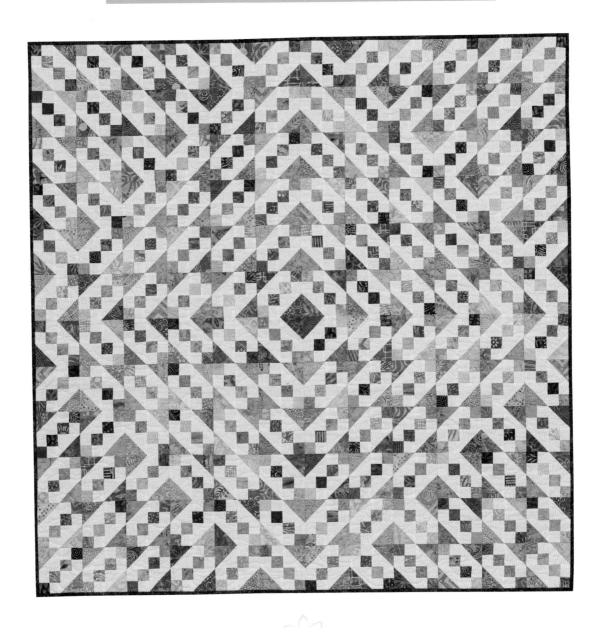

Pieced by Nancy Mahoney; quilted by Mary Frost

From *each* of the assorted dark batik squares, cut:

9 squares, 1½" × 1½" (576 total)

From the blue batik, cut:

6 strips, 2¼" × 42"

Limited Scrap Plan

While this quilt contains a lot of scraps, their placement is fairly easy. They are divided into just two groups: teal batiks (used for the triangles) and assorted bright batiks (used for the four patches). Choose the colors for the four patches randomly and your quilt is sure to sparkle.

Materials

Yardage is based on 42"-wide fabric.

- 2¼ yards of light batik for blocks
- 36 squares, 7" × 7" *each*, of assorted teal batiks for blocks
- 64 squares, 5" × 5" *each*, of assorted dark batiks for blocks
- ½ yard of blue batik for binding
- 3 yards of fabric for backing
- 55" × 55" piece of batting

Cutting

All measurements include ¼" seam allowances.

From the light batik, cut:

12 strips, 3" × 42"; crosscut into 144 squares, 3" × 3"

23 strips, 1½" × 42"; crosscut into 576 squares, 1½" × 1½"

From *each* of the assorted teal batik squares, cut:

4 squares, 3" × 3" (144 total)

Assembling and Finishing the Quilt

Press seam allowances in the directions indicated by the arrows.

1 Referring to "Making the Blocks" (page 59) for detailed instructions and illustrations, use the light, teal, and dark pieces to make 144 blocks.

Make 144 blocks, 4½" × 4½".

A New Twist

2 Lay out the blocks in 12 rows of 12 blocks each, rotating the blocks as shown in the quilt assembly diagram below to form a diamond shape in the center. Sew the blocks into rows and then join the rows. The quilt top should measure 48½" square, including seam allowances.

3 Stitch around the perimeter of the quilt top, ⅛" from the outer edges, to lock the seams in place.

4 Layer the quilt top with batting and backing; baste the layers together. Quilt by hand or machine. The quilt shown is machine quilted in an allover design of leaves and loops. Use the blue 2¼"-wide strips to make double-fold binding and then attach the binding to the quilt.

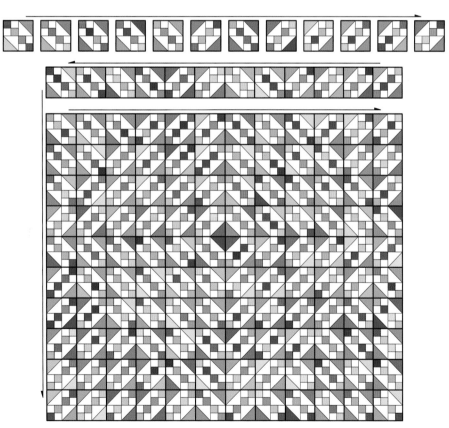

Quilt assembly

About the Author

As an author and teacher, Nancy has enjoyed making quilts for more than 40 years. An impressive range of her beautiful quilts has been featured in over 250 national and international quilt magazines.

This is Nancy's 15th book with Martingale. Her other best-selling books include *Learn to Paper Piece* (2016), *Simple Circles and Quick Curves* (2013), *Treasures from the '30s* (2010), and *Appliqué Quilt Revival* (2008).

When she's not designing and making quilts, Nancy enjoys traveling around the country, sharing her quilts, teaching her piecing and machine-appliqué techniques, and visiting gardens.

Nancy makes her home in central Georgia with her life partner of over 45 years, Tom, and their umbrella cockatoo, Prince.

Visit Nancy on her website at NancyMahoney.com and on Facebook at Nancy Mahoney Designs. Follow her on Instagram: @nancymahoneydesigns.